D0993945

Lancashire County Library

30118130411931

Boffin Boy and the Emperor's Tomb
by David Orme

Illustrated by Peter Richardson

Published by Ransom Publishing Ltd.
Unit 7, Brocklands Farm, West Meon, Hants. GU32 1JN
www.ransom.co.uk

ISBN   978 178127 050 9
First published in 2013
Reprinted 2015
Copyright © 2013 Ransom Publishing Ltd.

Illustrations copyright © 2013 Peter Richardson

A CIP catalogue record of this book is available from the British Library.

All rights reserved. No part of this publication may be reproduced, stored in a retrieval system, or transmitted, in any form or by any means, electronic, mechanical, photocopying, recording or otherwise, without the prior permission of the publishers.

The rights of David Orme to be identified as the author and of Peter Richardson to be identified as the illustrator of this Work have been asserted by them in accordance with sections 77 and 78 of the Copyright, Design and Patents Act 1988.

Design & layout: *redpaperdesign.co.uk*

Find out more about

Lancashire Library Services	
30118130411931	
PETERS	JF
£5.99	23-Apr-2015
EBU	

BOFFIN BOY
AND THE
EMPEROR'S
TOMB

By David Orme
Illustrated by Peter Richardson

Ransom

SECRET WAY IN

But does Boffin Boy know the password to open the door?

... past amazing treasures ...

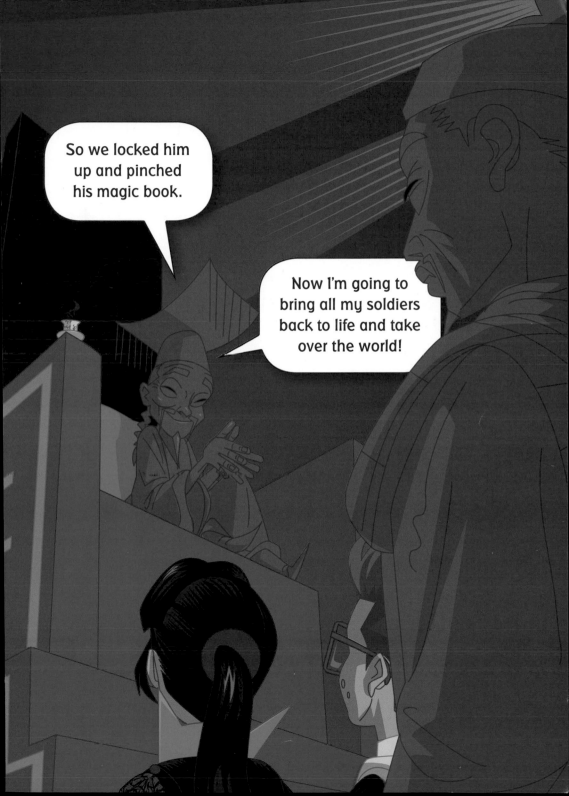

ABOUT THE AUTHOR

David Orme has written well over 200 books including poetry collections, fiction and non-fiction, and school text books. He especially likes writing science fiction stories, and historical stories set in London. Find out more at: www.magic-nation.com.